I had a bit too much to drink last night.

21st MARCH 2020

A couple of photos of me with my dog in the park.

Walking the dog.

24th March 2020

The Comedy Club in which I perform each Sunday in Glasgow is now closed due to lockdown, as is every other Club in the Country. I usually try to write some new material or the bones of a new joke/routine each week to try out at the Club on Sunday's. At first my thoughts were that this pleasure is now lost to me….well, it's a pleasure most of the time but sometimes I end up staring at a blank piece of paper and berating myself for not having a 'proper' job, while pressing my face against a window in frustration, no doubt disconcerting for people in the street who happen to be passing by my window at the time.

However, although I don't know how long the Clubs will be closed for, I thought I might as well continue with my joke writing routine and jot down some other observations and reflections as I have nothing else with which to occupy my time. Also, I live on my own and have no other distractions. I don't even have a cat.

26th March 2020

Today I'm reminded of the first joke I ever thought of while wandering around one evening in the area where I grew up in Dublin. I had no plans at the time to become a comedian and I don't really know why the joke came into my head. Having said that, all my heroes when I was growing up were steeped in comedy, from Groucho Marx to Peter Cook, Monty Python, and Flann O' Brien, the brilliant Irish humourist. A year later I found myself on the boat from Dublin to Holyhead en route to London to try my hand at the thriving comedy circuit there The joke is...."Like most people from Ireland, I was born a Catholic...which actual came a bit of a shock to my parents who were both Jewish."

The night after I'd thought of my first joke, I told it to my girlfriend at the time but she didn't see the humour in it.

"I don't see the humour in it", she said, shaking her head from side to side. We split up a couple of months later, not just because she didn't like my joke.

Regardless of my ex-girlfriends' reservations about the joke, I found myself a year later on the boat from Dun Laoghaire to Holyhead en route to London. So, I took the boat from Dublin to Holyhead and then a connecting train from Holyhead to London. ..well, sort of connecting because back then, I still don't know why they couldn't have co-ordinated things a bit better, but you had to wait for two hours in the port of Holyhead before the train arrived to take you to London-....two hours...in Holyhead...fucking Holyhead..you were all stuffed into this cold draughty soulless room for two hours....like a holding cell but even worse.....felt like a kind of dystopian hell with grey walls and colourless, really hard plastic seats which had become worn and cracked over the years from the weight of huge, agricultural Irish arses resting on them for two hours at a time waiting for the train to arrive....there wasn't even a dispensing machine .... children screaming, and a drunk from Co Leitrim with a huge tuft of red hair to match an even redder face singing, "The Wild Rover"....on the top of his voice...over and over again...but not in a continuous loop...that way you might have gotten used to it in some way. He'd sing for about twenty seconds and then forget the next verse and you'd be thinking..."Oh, thank fuck...that's the end of that", but then he'd start up again after another minute building up to the verse he'd forgotten in the hope that by singing it again the errant verse would just come back to him..."I've been a wild rover etc..whiskey and beer"....pause for 30 seconds or so...."I.ve been a wild..."......and then he just gave up and spewed all over the floor Everybody was just sitting in this cold draughty room in the port of Holyhead with the grey rain pelting against the windows for two hours from 11.30 at night till 1.30 the following morning waiting for the train to arrive. I don't remember much about the train journey but by the time I'd arrived in London Euston at six o' clock in the morning, I'd thought of another joke. I suppose it was inspired by the train journey from Holyhead to London.. The joke was ...and still is, I suppose...

"There's one thing I notice you have in England which we don't have in Ireland.....Birmingham."

I will write further in my Diary about arriving in London to perform stand up and settling into my grubby bedsit in Turnpike Lane.

2nd April 2020

A week has passed in lockdown and I have not succumbed to insanity, mild or otherwise, as yet. In fact, in a strange way I'm enjoying the fact that I don't have to put myself on the line every week in front of an audience.

I wrote a new joke today.

"I bumped into the ex-wife in the street recently. She's not actually my ex-wife...she's just called the ex-wife in our area because she's already been married nine times."

I think this is funny but writing a joke down is just the start of the process. The only sure-fire way to know if a joke works is to perform it in front of a live audience. I'm fairly sure that if I heard another comedian tell that joke, I would laugh. However, all comedians I know have written a joke only to discover an audience staring back at them with blank expressions when it's delivered to them. Fortunately, that doesn't happen too often, otherwise I would have given up long ago or have carried on until I was dragged away by other comedians or an audience

9th April 2020

My recurring nightmare of walking into my flat and discovering a giant Bishopper has flown in through an open window.

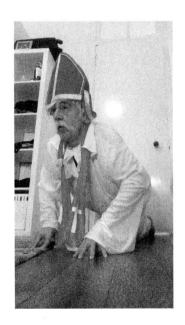

12th April 2020

I arrived in Euston station in London on a bleak Monday morning in January 1987 around 7am on the night train from Holyhead in Wales. I was carrying a suitcase with all my worldly belongings. It was one of those old fashioned suitcases without wheels and I cannot remember if the concept of suitcases with wheels had already been thought of by then or whether I just couldn't afford one. I knew that my first priority would be to find a very cheap flat somewhere and someone had advised me to head for Finsbury Park as there were ample flats to let in that area and it was only three stops or so on the Underground from

Euston.

I sat in a cafe in Finsbury Park trying to make a bland, milky coffee last for over an hour waiting for a nearby Estate Agents' to open.

Luckily they offered me a bedsit that same day in Turnpike Lane. You certainly wouldn't call it salubrious, a threadbare lime green sofa and a single rickety bed, but at least it looked out onto a small Park known as Ducketts' Common. But, I now had a base from which to kickstart my comedy career hopefully

13th April 2020

It's Easter Monday today!

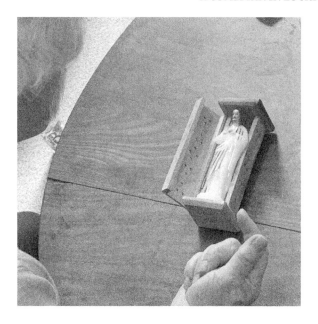

"C'mon Jesus....time to get up!"

16th April 2020

It's often been said to me that the chances of winning the Lottery are as good as approaching a complete stranger in the street and correctly guessing his or her phone number-....so, I've stopped doing that and started buying Lottery tickets instead.

It's a bit of a relief really as I often got some strange reactions from people who were reluctant to disclose their phone number.

21st April 2020

Before lockdown, I tended to only pay a visit to the super-market for provisions once or maybe twice per week. But since lockdown, it's become a form of a substitute social outlet. I would never have believed before that visiting the supermarket would become the highlight of my day. In that light, I have decided to keep an occasional diary of my visits to the supermarket.

Checkout Asst : Is it still sunny outside?

Me : Yeah, it's still very sunny.

Checkout Asst : I finish in ten minutes.

Me : Okay...so, will I just wait for you outside?

Checkout Asst : What?....no, I didn't mean.....I meant....

Me : Oh....

Checkout Asst: £13.49 when you're ready

28th April 2020

I've never grown a beard before so I thought I might grow one in lockdown to see what it looks like...what do you think?

3rd May 2020

I spotted this old lady standing on the other side of the street earlier today, looking a bit vulnerable. It was clear that she wanted to cross the street but she was looking very hesitant, so I thought I should walk over and help her across.

Then, a thought struck me....what if she's barking mad and thinks that I'm her ex-husband who left the house 36 years ago, saying he was just going out to buy cigarettes in the local shop but never bothered coming back. And for the past 36 years she has been building up this diatribe to shout at him if he ever decided to come back. Okay, after a day or two, she probably would have just rehearsed something along the lines of....' Where the bloody hell were you?'. But after 36 years....36 long years, a lot of bad things would have gone down. Was I prepared to have to listen to an endless rant detailing 36 years of bitterness, pain and struggle and how she hadn't been able to afford a new skirt since 1986 (I'm very observant and I could tell that the skirt she was wearing dated back to the mid 1980's). It was a bit of a dilemma for me, so I thought the best thing to do was to go for a quick coffee to have a think about it....I don't normally drink coffee but life can occasionally throw something at you which you've never had to deal with before. In the end I decided that I was making a mountain out of a molehill and went back to where she'd been standing. Fortunately, she was still there after ten minutes.

So, I started to help her across the street but halfway across, we discovered that I was actually older than her...so we swapped, and she helped me across the second half.

7th May 2020

While preparing myself a cup of tea earlier, I was reminded of my dislike of modern kettles and about a ritual I often used to practice on them.

You may wonder how anyone could develop a dislike of a kitchen utensil. Well, what I dislike about modern kettles is the way they turn themselves off when THEY"VE decided that the water is boiled. I was not prepared to put up with this! As soon as I put the switch on the kettle to ON, I used to place some masking tape over it to keep it in place so that the kettle can't turn itself off. Within minutes, the little bastard would be hoppin' up and down screaming for mercy, steam pouring everywhere. I would then place a kazoo on it's spout to increase the effect of its humiliation. I also used to sometimes put the kettle on, wait for the water to boil and then not bother making a cup of tea or coffee at all. Kettles hate that...all that effort for nothing.

I'm now thinking that I will revisit those rituals to amuse myself during lockdown.

I've also noticed myself lately staring venomously at my toaster which has been acting erratically recently. There must a similar way of exacting revenge on my toaster the next time it refuses to release a piece of toasted bread from its clutches and that by the time you finally do extract it, the slice of toast has been mutilated.

15th May 2020

There's one particular thing I've noticed as I've made my way through life…it's always surprising how paranoid someone at the top of a ladder becomes when a complete stranger like myself starts climbing up after him.

I can't pretend that's a new joke. In fact, it was the third joke I ever wrote. I can't be sure but I think I wrote it just a couple of days after arriving in London while wandering around the surroundings of Turnpike Lane. I spent most of my time each day trying to write new material while living off fish fingers and ginger nut biscuits.

This was 1987 and the comedy circuit in London was thriving at the time but wasn't as cluttered with hundreds of comedians as it is now so you didn't have to wait months and months to get a try out spot/open mic at the Clubs. In fact, one Club which I rang up offered me a spot the same night but I had to decline as I still only had four jokes in my repertoire. My office was a phone box just a couple of hundred yards from my bedsit. I would spend a couple of hours each day, spread over a few different shifts, ringing up comedy clubs and requesting an open spot. My first gig was at a place called The Tunnel Club. It was run by the legendary and irrepressible Malcolm Hardee and I was completely unaware at the time that the Club was notorious for comedians being booed off stage, often encouraged by Malcolm himself. But saying that makes it seem like Malcolm was unpleasant, which he really wasn't. The culture of the Club, curated by Malcolm, was that if the audience liked you, it could actually be the best gig in London. On the other hand, if they didn't like you, they certainly didn't hold back on their disapproval of your act, to put it mildly. It took me ages to find the Club that night as I was unfamiliar with London and in particular the area around Blackwall Tunnel. The Tunnel Club was in a function room of The Mitre pub which was located in a dimly lit street almost directly beneath the Blackwall Tunnel. The place seemed scarily sinister and threatening to me, not helped by the smell and sight of gas fumes from a nearby gasworks. I was tempted to turn back and retreat to the relative comfort of my bedsit in Turnpike Lane but I somehow managed to propel myself forward and walked through the doors. There were a group of guys playing pool or maybe snooker in the main area of the pub. To an over protected middle-class boy from South County Dublin, they all looked really dodgy. One of them detached himself from the others and approached me. Foolishly I thought he was going to threaten me in some way. The glasses he was wearing had thick lenses and in the dim light of the pub, I couldn't see his eyes properly. He was wearing a dark, shabby suit, with a tie which was loosened on his shirt.

" Alright mate? "

" I'm..looking for Malcolm. "

" That's me. "

" Oh, I'm Michael…I rang earlier about a gig "

" Yeah, recognised the accent…follow me mate, take you to dressing room.

He led me to a sort of dressing room and I think he may have even brought me a drink. He made me feel as relaxed as I could have been in the circumstances.

The Tunnel Club was noted for it's heckling culture but often the heckles were quite clever rather than just negative. I remember one act who'd been on the stage for about five minutes without any reaction of any nature when out of the blue someone from the audience shouted through the silence…."What do you want?". There is no comeback to a heckle like that if your act is crumbling and the only dignified thing to do is walk off stage, which is what the comedian in question did. I also remember one night that Malcolm had booked a mime artist to appear on the bill, not the sort of act you would expect to do well in the cauldron of the Tunnel Club, possibly the reason Malcolm booked him in the first place. The mime artist only lasted a couple of minutes when someone shouted…"I'm blind, tell us a joke". Possibly cruel but still very clever. I was booked to do five minutes that first night and I survived without being heckled or booed off. I really don't know why I wasn't heckled because my act didn't go down very well. I wouldn't say that I died on my arse but I was lucky to survive unscathed.

I consider myself luckier in some ways to other comedians during lockdown in that I receive a State pension and I am not totally dependent on my earnings from working as a comedian.

The big advantage of being a pensionable age is that you get paid every month simply for not being dead. Of course, the disadvantage of being a pensioner is that you are officially old….you can no longer pretend that 'deaths' door' is in the far distant future. However, I am not afraid of dying when the time comes...I have a bigger fear of NOT dying. Don't get me wrong, I have no desire to die at the moment as I'm quite happy with my lot. (well, most of the time anyway). But I suffer from an underlying fear of reaching 102/103 years old and thinking to myself..."Shit!, this is beginning to drag on a bit now and to make matters worse my 79 year old son is still living at home. I've been nagging him for years to clean his bedroom but he says he can't do it because of his arthritis."

19th May 2020

It is not a well known fact that before balloons were invented, people used to blow up aubergines to celebrate a birthday or special occasion!

Blowing up aubergines for a party!

24th May 2020

It's not just that nuns look like penguins. I saw one today slip a small herring into her mouth from the counter in a fish shop, swallow it before the fishmonger noticed and then quickly waddle out of the shop.

28th May 2020

It's raining quite heavily outside today but I'd planned to go for a long cycle on my bike. So, I thought what the hell, I'd planned to go for a cycle, so I'm going to go for one regardless.

Here I am taking in the sights of my flat as I cycle back and forth from my hallway to the kitchen.

4th June 2020

I've decided to amuse myself today by standing at my window and allowing passers by on the street outside to think there is a giant living in the house.

7th June 2020

I suppose a milestone in any comedians life is the first time you really die on stage....I mean, really die when nobody, not one person in the audience, is either laughing or even smiling at anything you say...just total silence...you can see some people looking at you as if to say..."Please stop now and just go away" and other more sensitive ones just looking at the ground in embarrassment for you, and you've already told your best joke but the audience are still just staring blank faced at you and you can feel your hands starting to shake slightly and your mouth goes completely dry, you start sweating and smelling of fish fingers and as you finally walk off stage you can feel the relief coming off everyone in the room. I can't remember the actual venue where I had my first death. I'd only been in London less than two months at the time but it was a pub somewhere in South London, I think, can't remember the name of the venue...maybe I've blanked it out. But I do remember the aftermath. It's not just an emotional reaction...it's also like being punched in the stomach..there's an actual physical ache, and I remember lying on my treasured sofa bed for most of the next day in a foetal position, staring into the abyss. But you can't lie on your sofa bed for days on end feeling sorry for yourself..those fish fingers don't cook themselves....that was undoubtedly the lowest point so far. I remember sitting in my bedsit that following evening...actually eating a Birds' Eye chilli con carne because I'd decided I needed a change from fishfingers...chili con carne was tasteless by the way.

As a culinary tip, I don't recommend Birds Eye chilli con carne. But as I was sitting there eating the tasteless chilli con carne and watching snooker on my black and white television because a button or dial had broken off on the TV and it was stuck on BBC1 and that's all I could watch...I was thinking of just going out for a walk or something but then afraid that if I did go out I might bump into someone who'd been at the gig the night before. I knew it was time to either chuck it all in and go back home or decide to really go for it.. .thinking, 'it can't get any fucking worse or more grim than this'. And two days later I had this Eureka moment...I realise that the word, "Eureka" doesn't really match my facial expression, but I used to spend a lot of the day just wandering around the streets where I lived, partly to get away from the grim lonely bedsit but it sometimes helped to free my mind to write comedy material. But two days after my first big death on stage, I was walking along this street, it was a very well to do area...lots of big detached houses in their own grounds. It had been raining and I was wearing a long rain mac. Not long after the rain had stopped I remember going by one particular house and the front garden was festooned with all these amazing, exotic looking flowers and the scent coming off them was just amazing after all the rain. I was just drawn into the garden because I was used to the grotty surrounds of my bedsit and this sort of looked like paradise. I suppose I looked a bit menacing just standing there in my rain mac, my big mane of dark hair dripping wet, matted to my head, bending over some strangers flower bed. I'd only been in the garden a couple of minutes, I mean, I hadn't encroached very far...maybe 10/ 15 yards into the garden...and I was walking by the flower beds when the front door of the house opened and a woman started shouting...

" Hey you...what are you doing in my garden? "...
I was about to say something like..."nothing sinis-

ter..just admiring your flower bed", or something similar, when I saw this huge fucking Dobermann dog bounding out through the front door and heading towards me . I quickly ran out of the garden. But there was some guy walking by at the time who'd witnessed the entire incident and he thought the whole thing was hilarious... and that planted a seed in my mind. At that time, I used to wear a long mac and walk on stage holding a plastic supermarket bag and that in itself garnered laughs from the audience. Following the incident in the garden I began to open with the line...."People often say to me...hey you, what are you doing in my garden?" The joke was later to be plagiarised by the comedian, Joe Pasquale, on the Royal Variety Command Show, and then made slightly famous when the comedian, Stewart Lee, picked up on it and created a very funny routine about it, lampooning Joe Pasquale.

10th June 2020

My mother was born on the 10th of June which springs to mind a phrase or rather a threat that she used to employ whenever myself or one of my brothers' were misbehaving. She never hit us that I can recall but would often threaten that she would…"Beat you to within an inch of your life." However, when metric replaced imperial it placed her at a severe disadvantage…." I'll beat you to within an….an……." but by the time she'd converted into metric, we'd already scarpered.

16th June 2020

Now that I have sometime on my hands, I finally found time to put this to the test!

21st June 2020

As I've mentioned before, my only social outlets at the moment (if they can be called that) are my regular visits to the supermarket. In this regard, I have often found myself in conversation with the resident butcher in the supermarket who could be described as garrulous.

I discovered today that he is not just simply opposed to vegetarianism or indeed veganism. I would suggest he harbours a pathological hate of anyone who has chosen a vegetarian or vegan diet.

He had run his own Family Butchers' for a number of years but due to a fall in custom which he blames on the 'rising tide of vegetarianism', he was forced to close his shop and take up a job in the supermarket. He regards this as a drop in status on a catastrophic scale and points the finger at all vegetarians/vegans for his misfortune.

Me: Morning.

Butcher : See that fella there!

Me; Where?

Butcher : That eejit at the deli counter buying chick peas

Me; Eh…

Butcher: The one wearing the hand knitted jumper.

Me: Yeah, what about him?

Butcher: A vegetarian, that's what about him. Thinks he's a cut above me…always walks by my counter with a snooty look on his face as if I was made of muck.

Me : Are you sure, maybe you're mistaken..it could be just…

Butcher : Of course, I'm sure. Wouldn't be surprised if he's a vegan as well.

Me: Well, quite a few people are beginning to follow a vegan lifestyle.

Once I'd uttered these words, I immediately regretted it.

Butcher: Who are you telling, breeding like rabbits, they are…vegan this, vegan that. You can hardly turn your head without a vegan appearing beside you.

Me: Well, I think maybe that's a bit of an exaggeration.

Butcher: An exaggeration, my granny. Mark my words, they're everywhere....anyway, what can I get you?

Me: Oh nothing, I was just passing when you called me over. Going to have some fish for dinner tonight.

Butcher : Lord save us!

27th June 2020

When I find myself with thyme-like stubble, Hairy Mary comes to me, Holding out a scissors, Cut it free.

Yes, I have a lot of time on my hands at the moment!

3rd July 2020

Proof, if proof were ever needed, that the Dalai Lama is a fraud and was never a real Llama.

9th July 2020

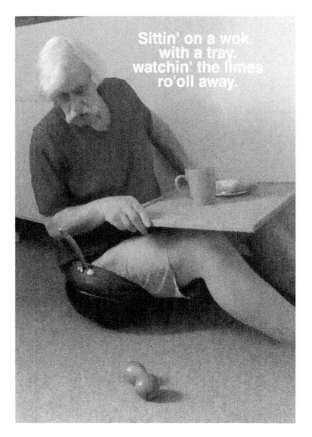

I'm reliably told that this was the first draft for the lyrics of "Sittin' on the dock of the bay."

11th July 2020

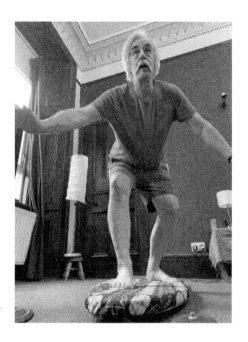

Lockdown surfing

12th July 2020

Today is the traditional day for Orange marches around Scotland and Northern Ireland. No marches this year because of Covid but here is a photo I took of a march I joined in with last year.

What a laugh I had!

What a crazy, wacky shower of japesters Orangemen are!!!

14th July 2020

There is a resident busker outside my local supermarket. I suspect that he is there most days because he is always there on my tri-weekly shopping visits. The guy has no musical talent at all, singing badly out of tune and often hitting the wrong chords on his guitar. Despite this, he performs with great passion and is always at his post even when the weather is particularly unpleasant. We engage with each other on friendly, nodding terms and I make a point of dropping 50p or so into his hat each time.

Today I was feeling a bit more generous than usual because I had just received payment for some work I had performed which had turned out to be a little more lucrative than I thought it would be. His favourite song to play is 'Love me do' by The Beatles and he was in full flow when I opened my wallet and dropped what I thought was a five pound note into his hat. Well, I did drop a five pound note into his hat but I hadn't noticed that a twenty pound note which had become slightly wedged to the five pound note inside my wallet came out with it as well and both had reached the interior of his hat before I realised what had happened. I was going to retrieve the twenty pound note, explaining it was an accident but his eyes had lit up with such surprise and gratitude when he saw twenty five pounds landing in his hat that I couldn't bring myself to do so.

He immediately stopped playing to express his thanks and insisted that I request a song of my choice which he would play for me on the spot. I couldn't think of anything off hand but I suppose because he'd been playing a Beatles song, I blurted out, "Eleanor Rigby".

He seemed a little unsure at first for a few seconds as if he was rehearsing the tune in his head, going over the lyrics to see if he could remember them. He then nodded to himself, struck a chord on his guitar and launched himself into ' Eleanor Rigby'.

Well, the chords he was playing vaguely matched the tune of 'Eleanor Rigby' but his lyrics were from 'Lucy in the sky'.

"Picture yourself on a boat on the river,

With tangerine trees and marmalade skies…"

(slight pause)…Father McKenzie writing the words of a

sermon

That no one will hear,

No one comes near....

Lucy in the sky with diamonds,

Lucy in the sky with diamonds,

All the lonely people......"

He carried on for a full four minutes, unintentionally morphing the lyrics of Eleanor Ribgy and Lucy In The Sky . I had little choice but to stand, watch and listen to him since he was playing for my personal delectation. I occasionally nodded in appreciation whenever he looked toward me to gauge my reaction but all I was thinking was that I had paid twenty pounds, which I could ill afford, to endure his painful rendition of the two iconic songs from the Beatles catalogue.

I thanked him once he'd mercifully reached the end and I entered the supermarket with a very heavy heart and £20 poorer than I'd planned.

Elderly Woman : Excuse me, young man?

Me : Me?

Elderly Woman : Yes, I wonder would you mind reaching up and fetching me one of those yellow bags of tea.

Me : Yeah sure...I'm not that young though!...would you prefer if I gave you a leg up?

Elderly Woman : A leg up…..

Me : Sorry, I was just being silly.

Elderly Woman : No, I'd enjoy that.

Me : You sure?

Elderly Woman : Absolutely….

So, I hooshed her up on one leg as gingerly as I could and she fetched the packet of yellow tea bags.

Elderly Woman : Thank you….I haven't had a leg up in a long time.

Me : No problem.

Elderly Woman : I'm here most Tuesdays!

With that information in mind, I headed to the Butchers' section to buy a couple of pork chops on the bone.

Me : Morning, I'll have two of your pork chops please.

Butcher : Started raining, I see.

Me : Yes.

Butcher : Right, two pork chops coming up....do you know how many vegans I've seen in here today already?

Me : Em...no.

Butcher : Twelve.

Me : How did you know they were vegans?

Butcher : How do you think?

I decided not to rise to his question as I sensed he was primed to unleash a barrage of information on how to recognise a vegan on sight.

Butcher : A friend of mine was telling me that in some parts of the Middle East, vegans are banned from supermarkets.

Me : Really, that doesn't sound...

Butcher : And launderettes.

Me : Why, supermarkets and launderettes?

Butcher : Oh, who knows. They have some strange laws in some of those countries.

Me : Did your friend lend you any further insight into this unlikely scenario?...it doesn't really make any sense.

Butcher : I don't know...maybe there were a few incidents involving vegans.

Me : In supermarkets and launderettes?

Butcher : Who knows....there you go, two pork chops.

17th July 2020

Having put my first big death on stage behind me….well, not quite behind me because no comedian forgets that completely (it's memory is just lurking somewhere in the back of your brain, ready to assert itself at any time it feels the need), I discovered that the more gigs I did the better I became and I began to develop a good twenty minute set. I'd been in London for eight months or so when I wrote what was to become my signature joke which was largely based on a true story. I was in a pub near where I lived in Turnpike Lane one evening. I was on my own as I still hadn't really got to know anyone in London. I'd just ordered a drink at the bar when a guy standing beside me said…."Excuse me, mate, are you from Dublin?", I said, "I am, yeah."..he then said, "Oh, do you know a bloke called Sean Corcoran?"…I mean, there were over one million people living in Dublin even back then but the really annoying thing was, I bloody did know a bloke called Sean Corcoran. I recently posted this joke/story on twitter and to my surprise it seemed to resonate with many people and actually went viral with over 360,000 hits. A year or so later, I was to perform in a show at the Edinburgh Fringe Festival with Jo Brand and Kevin Day titled… "Sean Corcoran and Phyllis

Holt present." Jo had a very funny joke about someone she knew named Phyllis Holt and that's where the show got its title.

The biggest prize to aim for on the comedy circuit in London was to receive a booking at The Comedy Store. I waited over a year before I even attempted to ask for a try out spot there. I went down to the Comedy Store one Saturday evening to do a try out spot. I'd learned from other comedians that the guy who booked the acts was a man named Kim Kinnie, who was later to become my mentor and friend. Luckily I went down a storm and Kim offered me a booking...a fully paid booking at the Comedy Store for three weeks later.. I walked home on air.

Since then, I have been lucky enough to earn a living as a stand up comedian.

20th July 2020

Here's my hot tip for the day should you ever find yourself

in this situation…..

When someone across the street from you waves in your direction and you wave back to them before realising they're waving to someone behind you…hide your embarrassment by running across the street and rugby-tackling them to the ground so they're the ones who look stupid, not you.

24th July 2020

Looks like I've finally achieved my ambition to be part of the cast of Riverdance.

30th July 2020

I came across some photos today dating back a few years ago when I was on holiday in Spain with my girlfriend at the time. We decided to hire a car for a few days. I remember the car hire agent asking me if I'd ever driven on the right hand side of the road before. He seemed a little unsettled when I told him only once or twice before back in Ireland when I was a bit pissed.

I can recall a Government Drink Drive campaign in Ireland in the seventies. The mainstay of the campaign was a large poster with a line of 5 pints of lager across it, but there was a X against the fifth pint and the tag line was...."Stay away from that fifth pint."

There also used to be a sort of community advice programme on RTE called Garda Patrol. It aired a couple of minutes before the main 6 0' clock news if I remember correctly. But I vividly remember watching one at the time of the Drink Drive campaign. A Garda Sergeant was appealing to the public about the dangers of drink driving and this is what he said, word for word....

"If you've driven to the pub and plan to drive home but can't remember how many pints you've had, just have a couple more at the most and leave it at that."

I'm not glorifying it, but the set up was much different back then. If you were driving along and accidentally mounted the pavement, clipping a pedestrian on the leg, you'd just hop out of the car and say…"Sorry about that, mate, I'm a bit pissed.", and he'd say "Ah fair enough, as long as it wasn't on purpose."

I admit that I used to drink and drive, smoke while I was driving and sometimes have sex with my girlfriend, all at the same time….it's just as well there were no mobiles phones back, it would have been mayhem. There were no mobile phones then, no internet, no X-Box games and so on….to be honest, I'm not even sure if Soup of the Day was around then, back in the good 'ol days before soups became competitive…when a hearty vegetable broth didn't have to compete on a menu with something like, Spicy Moroccan butternut squash…I still remember when pork used to be pork before people started pulling it, and there no different types of coffee, only one type, it was called a cup of coffee, and if you went into a cafe and ordered something like a skinny latte and a panini with sun dried tomatoes and mozzarella, they probably would have disappeared round the back and called the police....."There's a strange man in our cafe making up odd words."

There were no vegetarians in Ireland back then either....they'd all been sent to London by their parents so they wouldn't bring shame on the family. There was a bigger taboo then in Ireland about being vegetarian than there was about being gay, which has carried on to this day. Gay marriage is now legal in Ireland but vegetarians are still not allowed to marry each other in Ireland.

So, as I mentioned, we didn't have X-Box games or the internet to amuse ourselves with, so we had to make our own fun, but it was usually shite.....like finding a snail on the path in your back garden and turning it the other way round to see how long it took to realise that it was going in the wrong direction.

Mind you, occasionally we did have some fun...

'Kidnap the Jehovah Witness' was a good game we often played if there were Jehovah Witnesses targeting our street. When you opened the front door to a Jehovah Witness, you'd tell him that your mother has just fallen down the steps leading to the cellar and would he help out. Once he'd stepped down into the cellar, you'd immediately lock the door behind him. Of course, it wasn't a real kidnapping as there was no ransom involved. It was just a bit of fun and you'd always let him out after a few hours once he'd agreed to become a Catholic.

3rd August 2020

"Does my nun look big in this?"

5th August 2020

I was idling away some time today looking through some of my old diaries in which I used to note down all my gig dates for the year or anything relevant to my life as a comedian.

This is an entry I made in my Diary on the 5th August from the year 1994.

'Last night I was doing a gig at the Bloomsbury Theatre in London. It had been billed as a night of comedy featuring Irish comedians who were working on the London comedy circuit. The bill included myself, Ardal O'Hanlon, and Dylan Moran. I was standing in the foyer of the Theatre after the gig chatting to Ardal when we were approached by a couple of guys who introduced themselves as Graham and Arthur. They mentioned that they were writing a sitcom about priests on an island in the West of Ireland and had both of us in mind for different parts in the show.'

I have to be honest that when I heard it was about priests on an almost deserted island off the west coast, I thought it might be some traditional stereo typed version of the Ireland which I had happily left behind me. How wrong I was! A couple of months later I was called in by Hat Trick productions to audition for the part of Father Stone in Father Ted. I remember Graham and Arthur were present along with the show's producer, Geoffrey Perkins. I learned later that Geoffrey Perkins wasn't sure if I was the right one for the part until I delivered the line to Father Ted (I think Graham was reading F. Ted's dialogue) "Well, yeah...if there's a fire.", in response to Ted's pleas for me to leave the house.

A few months later, I found myself on set filming the episode in Teddington Studios in London for the indoor shots and then filming for three days in the West of Ireland for the outside shots. Happy days!

7th August 2020

It is a huge misconception that the existence of leprechauns in Ireland has always been a myth. This may seem like a random statement but I mention it in view of some startling and disturbing news emanating from a remote area in Ireland. Before I impart this news to you, it is important for you to know that leprechauns did exist in Ireland over 400 years ago. It is estimated that the leprechaun population at that time was around 2000, however gradually over the years the leprechauns slowly and irrevocably began to evolve into jockeys and have since become extinct. I have it on good authority that 'jockey' DNA shows distinct traces of 'leprechaun' DNA. How can experts determine the DNA of leprechauns, I hear you shout? Well, as evidenced by the photograph below, a grave of a long dead leprechaun was revealed fairly recently when it was disturbed by localised flooding due to a particularly heavy rainfall. It was not long before scientists were able to establish it's DNA from it's bones. Naturally, the leprechauns' traditional dress has become badly discoloured over the years and you can also see the remains of it's shillelagh lying in front of the leprechaun on it's left.

The reason I mention all this is because I have received information about a 'jockey trafficking' racket emanating from a remote part of Ireland. I was unaware that there was a small hidden village in the South West of Ireland known as 'Jockeytown', which is home to over 240 jockeys, mostly Irish, but jockeys of any Nationality are apparently welcome to reside there. Naturally all the buildings in the town are of a smaller dimension than standard buildings and although outsiders are allowed to visit the town it is difficult for anyone over 5ft, 4" to negotiate entry and exit from a shop or the local pub where the bar stools are also of such a miniature nature that someone of standard build would find their arse protruding crudely over both sides. Because of this, tourists to the the local pub in Jockeytown tend to remain standing, and by necessity adopting a stooped posture.

I am told that at least 12 jockeys have already been smuggled out of the Country to the USA for super wealthy Irish Americans who keep them in captivity and show them off to their friends as living leprechauns.

Here is a recent photo of jockeys in Jockeytown meeting to discuss the crisis among their numbers.

10th August 2020

I had a dream last night that my busker friend had been 'discovered' overnight, become a youtube sensation and was selling out stadiums around the Country. However, he hadn't forgotten my generosity in dropping a £20 note into his hat and had repaid my generosity by paying off my mortgage,

Any doubts that it was a dream were dispelled as I approached the supermarket and he was standing in his usual position re-tuning his guitar in between songs. I'd already decided to come straight with him and just ask for my £20 back as I could ill afford it. I walked straight up to him.

Busker : Ah, good to see you, been bursting to tell you something…

Me : Oh really, I've also been hoping to…

Busker : That £20 you put in my hat…

Me : Yes, that's what I....

Busker : Managed to buy some new strings for my guitar with it.....it's like having a new guitar, I can't thank you enough.

Me : Oh...it's....that's....great.

Busker : It's like a new lease of life.

Me : Great....well, best of luck.

In the circumstances I couldn't really ask him for my twenty pounds back and I suppose the fact that it had given him such joy, it took the sting out of my loss.

13th August 2020

I'm sure that most of you like me have often wondered why cows always looked so disgruntled and pissed off with their lot.

Well, due to extensive research on my part, I can now reveal the reason why cows are not happy animals.

In the greater scheme of things, cows were around on earth thousands of years before horses or greyhounds made an appearance.....and people used to RACE COWS back then.

That is precisely the reason why cows always looked so pissed off these days, because the natural instinct of the cow is to race....it's just that they're fairly shit at it.

You can tell they are not contented animals from the sounds they make....a long plaintive moan....."Moooooo-ooo!......Mooooooo!...."......easily translated to..." I'm pissed of....I want to race."

In the photograph which I've presented, you can see the cows longing back to the old days when they would line up for a race.

21st August 2020

I've written a new routine explaining the origins of Irish dancing which was triggered by a clip I saw recently on television.

As most of you will be aware, Irish dancing does not involve any movement of the arms. The reason for this is because Irish dancing was first ' invented ' involuntarily in the west of Ireland in the late eighteenth century by a woman named Kitty Ni Houlihan. The story is that Kitty had no arms, so if she was talking animatedly to someone and wanted to emphasise what she was saying by gesticulating, she was compelled to gesticulate with her legs instead. Many people in her village found this very unsettling and after a while it was decided that she was probably a witch. So, one day she was taken by some of the townsfolk to the nearby river and thrown in to see if she would sink. But she didn't sink and kept herself afloat by kicking her legs about like nobodys' business. She was swept downstream, still kicking her legs about like there was no tomorrow....and that's how Riverdance first acquired its name!

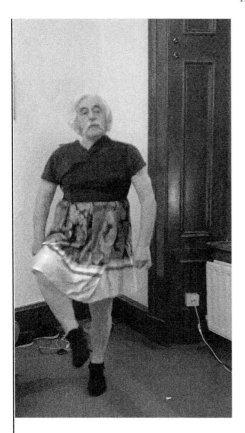

Here I am ' riverdancing ' the arse out of lockdown

28th August 2020

Here's a little tip for some of you. Impress the ladies with your level of oral hygiene by wearing a toothbrush and toothpaste in your breast pocket instead of a kerchief.

I like my women like I like my tea, because i don't really like coffee…to be honest with you.

6th September 2020

Here's a tip for the next time you're attending a funeral....wear your trousers at half mast as a mark of respect.

8th September 2020

Finally managed to swing some finance for a second ironing board...one for weekdays and one for the weekend.

11th September 2020

It seems my story about jockey trafficking to the USA is true. A sensational blog from a man in Philadelphia who wishes to remain anonymous,but has close links with the FBI, tells the harrowing story of two jockeys who managed to escaped from their captivity and are now under the protection of the Federal Bureau. The man claims that the FBI are keeping the whole issue secret at the moment and have not yet disclosed any information on the plight of the jockeys to the press or media. However, he has managed to acquire an artists' impression of the two jockeys following their escape and journey into the safe hands of the FBI.

One of the jockeys who is named Seamus, although it is not yet clear if that is his real name or a pseudonym, relates his story in the man's blog.

" *We must have been drugged with somethin'*

fierce altogether 'cos all is remember is wakin' up in this big basement somewhere. It was oney later we discovered we were in a big mansion in some American's house. We still didn't know den dat we were in America....we tought dat it was just some house in Ireland owned by an American fella. Mother of Jaysus you could have knocked us all over with a matchstick when we heard we were in America. We'd still no idea den what lay ahead of us. It was eider de next day or de day after dat...I can't be sure 'cos sure weren't we still reelin' under de effects of de drugs dey'd given us, meself and annuder jockey, were marched into....God above what would ye call it?....a sort of indoor area, I suppose. We were both given a shilelegh each and told to start batterin' the shite out of each udder-....and weren't dere fellas in suits sittin' outside a glass partition ting roarin' us on. Didn't dey have bets on which one of us would win and down the udder one with a smack of the shilelagh....it was terrible....terrible altogether!...

Anyway, after four long weeks of dis, didn't meself and John Jo manage to escape. I won't be

A COMEDIAN IN LOCKDOWN

tellin' ya now how we did it 'cos the udder fellas still in captivity might want to try the same ting as us and I don't want to give the game away like.

85

16th September 2020

If you watch the National 6 o' clock news on BBC, you will know that before the camera pans on to the newscaster, it first shows a panoramic view of the newsroom with nearly all the staff at their desks. But there is also a woman walking through the newsroom wearing a brown shoulder bag on her way to her desk.....I slept with her once. I don't like to brag about these things but if you've slept with someone who's on the national news everyday, it's very hard to keep it to yourself.

I think her name was Christine but I could be wrong. But I vividly remember walking into her bathroom at some point and noticing that she used euthymol toothpaste. Definitely a bit weird, I thought....I mean, who uses euthymol toothpaste? I'm not sure why but serial killers spring to mind. I can imagine Ted Bundy using euthymol toothpaste and definitely Fred West, you can tell.

I think we were supposed to go out with each other again

the following week but then I thought to myself....euthymol toothpaste! I could wake up in the morning tied to her bedpost with her leaning over me about to force feed me tube after tube of euthymol toothpaste through one of those nozzles used for piping cream onto cakes.

19th September 2020

Here's another little tip for you if find yourself with time on your hands during the day.

Wander about using your rucksack as a baby sling with a dolls' head sticking out at the top.

22nd September 2020

I'm having what is commonly called a bad hair day. The minute I woke up this morning, I realised there was something amiss with my hair and soon surmised that it's PH Balance had shifted overnight and to make matters worse I couldn't find any shampoo in my bathroom that promised to restore the PH Balance.

I had to make do with a shampoo with light reflecting technology combined with intelligent microbes. This was at least some consolation. Having to spend the day with my hairs' PH Balance in disarray and not even having intelligent microbes to compensate, simply doesn't bear thinking about.

29th September 2020

Todays' quiz....Which one is the real Albert Einstein?

30th September 2020

I've decided to paint a moustache on the outside of my mask so that people I know will still recognise me in the street.

2nd October 2020

As I approach the supermarket today, I see the busker standing outside ' regaling ' people entering the supermarket. He spots me when I am about twenty yards away and greets me with a huge grin on his face. As I come up to him, I drop what had been my customary 50p into his hat. He tried to maintain the grin on his face but it was clear that he was disappointed with the paltry amount compared to the windfall he had received from me the last time.

I hadn't planned to buy chicken wings today in the supermarket but they looked quite tempting as I was passing the deli counter.

Me : Can I have four of the chicken wings, please

Deli Assistant: Sure, plain ones or with barbecue sauce?

Me: Just plain, please......

Deli Assistant: There you go!

Me : Thanks,....chicken wings are a bit of an anomaly, aren't they?

Deli Assistant : What's that?

Me : Well, the fact that chickens have wings but they still can't fly...they must wonder why they have wings in the first place, probably envying other birds flying about from tree to tree,migrating to far off exotic places, but no matter how hard they flap their wings, they still remain on the ground. I suppose it's a bit like...

Deli Assistant : Sorry, Sir, there are other customers waiting

....

Checkout Assistant : Mmmm, chicken wings, one of my favourites.

Me : Yeah, nice alright. I was just saying to the guy who served me at the deli counter, isn't it strange why chickens have wings that they can't use.

Checkout Assistant : Suppose....hadn't really thought about that.

Me : Bit like...maybe, rabbits having arms they can't use.... just get in their way if they're trying to run back into their warren to escape from a predator.

Checkout Assistant : Yes, will that be all for you today?

Me : Yes, thanks

Checkout Assistant : £18.24 when you're ready please.

10th October 2020

When you wake from a nightmare that your hoover is about to attack you and suck the breath from your body, and then realise it isn't a nightmare.

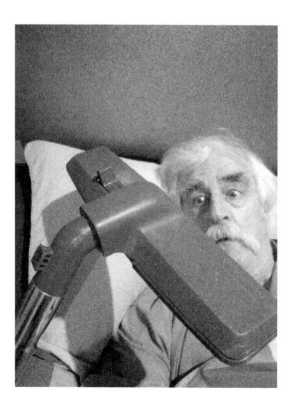

MICHAEL REDMOND

18th October 2020

If my previous story about rise of ' jockey smuggling ' in Ireland wasn't enough for you to appreciate the plight of some jockeys in the modern world, surely this recent statistic from the International Jockeys' Association will make you sit up and think.

The Association has revealed that over 30 jockeys have gone missing over the last five years. This is not as a result of jockey smuggling or trafficking but due to the garish outfits that jockeys wear, like bright yellow top sprinkled with red stars coupled with purple pantaloons, because apparently they are very vulnerable to large birds of prey as they're racing around a course on their horses…they're just plucked from their horses by a giant eagle or similar and never seen again. If you ever watch horse racing on television, you'll sometimes see a horse crossing the finishing line without any jockey on it…..Birds of Prey!

In this photo taken a couple of years near the Curragh race course in Ireland, you can just about see a small jockey being taken to his fate by a huge bird of prey.

30th October 2020

Butcher : You won't bloody believe it!

Me : What's that?

Butcher : My wife…

Me : Your wife?

Butcher : You won't believe it.

Me : What's happened….is she okay?

Butcher : No, not all.

Me : Oh, I'm very sorry, what's the….

Butcher : She's become a vegan. Told me last night, couldn't believe it….21 years together and she comes out with this, out of the blue…tells me while I was eating a sirloin steak, couldn't finish it, sticking in my throat it was. I'd no idea, no warning…she was even eating sausages last Tuesday.

Me : Well, I'm sure you can…

Butcher : Apparently it's not even grounds for a divorce.

Me : A divorce??

Butcher : If your wife becomes a vegan, it's not grounds for a divorce these days.

Me : I don't think that was ever the case....a change of dietary habits being cited as grounds for a divorce.

Butcher : A vegan...my wife...can you imagine?....anyway, what can I get you?

Me : Oh nothing today, thanks. I was just passing by when you called me over.

As I moved away from the butchers' counter, Jacko stormed into the back area and I heard the sound of a butchers' axe being brought down with unnecessary force onto a butchers' table. Although I didn't share his views and attitudes towards vegans, a small part of me felt sorry for him.

Me : Oh, hello stranger!

Other Shopper : Eh...I'm sorry, I can't quite place you.

Me : No, we're strangers

Other Shopper : ...Well, better be getting on....

3rd November 2020

When a dead person is referred to as…" The late " somebody or other, it always seems to me to be very unfair to expect them to be on time in the circumstances.

5th November 2020

When you forget why you walked into your shower cubicle in the first place, then suddenly remember, but forget to take your clothes off before turning the shower on.

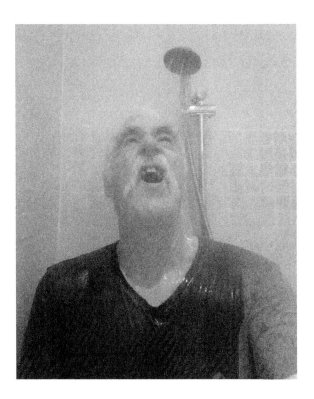

8th November 2020

I had occasionally noticed my neighbour who lives in a flat across the street from me as we went about our daily lives over the past few years. She lives in a flat on the first floor of her building as I do on mine and the windows of our living rooms face each other.

It was a coincidence that we both happened to be cleaning our windows at the same time. However, I wasn't wearing my glasses at the time and mistook the movement of her hand across her window as a wave towards me which I returned with gusto. She kindly returned the wave but it was clear that she had not initiated the social greeting. We then nodded awkwardly to each other.... well, at least my nod certainly possessed a degree of clumsiness because in my slight sense of social awkwardness my head had moved three times, two of them being involuntary movements precipitated by the first. I'm not sure if she had actually finished cleaning her window or if she'd decided to finish it later but she then closed her window and as she began to turn away I stupidly smiled towards her. I don't know if she didn't see my smile or chose to ignore it but she definitely didn't return one.

12th November 2020

Some people like to curl up on their sofa of an evening and watch television. I prefer to sit atop my ladder and take in the vista of my sitting room.

14th November 2020

Maybe in future, I should convert my dreams into some kind of business venture. My busker friend has actually become a you tube sensation. The person who posted the video of him singing Beatles songs with the lyrics of Lucy in the Sky mixed up to the tune of Eleanor Rigby may well have meant it as a joke. But either way, it's gone viral, as they say. Apparently it's received over a million hits on You Tube and I don't know if it's true or not but it's been said that Paul Mc Cartney loves the video..

I wish the busker well and who knows, I might even get my twenty quid back in the end.

16th November 2020

I bumped into the woman across the street from me in the supermarket today. The woman with whom I'd had minor social contact a few days earlier when I'd mistakenly thought she was waving at me as we both cleaned our windows.

Me : Oh, hello.

Woman : Hello…I'm trying to….

Me : I live across the street from you, we…

Woman : Oh sorry, yes of course, you waved at me when we were cleaning our windows the other day.

Me : Yes, I thought you had waved first but I think it was just your window cleaning action…not that it really matters….I suppose.

Woman : (smiling) No, not really…I'm Maureen.

Me : Michael, pleased to meet you.

Maureen : I know Maureen sounds a bit like someones' Auntie's name…never liked it.

Me : Oh, well….are you anyone's aunty?

Maureen: Yeah, I've a niece and a nephew.

Me : Well, there you are…you've grown into your name.

There was a slight pause and I thought for a split second, she was offended and didn't like my playful remark….but then she broke into a wide smile.

Maureen : Well…maybe see you next time we're cleaning our windows.

Me : Okay….what day do you usually clean them?

Maureen : Usually Wednesdays!….around 2 or 3 o'clock.

She walked away smiling and I wasn't really sure whether or not we'd made a tentative date, albeit one that would be conducted at a distance from across the street.

18th November 2020

I remember I once managed to talk someone down who was standing on a window ledge on the 11th floor of a high rise building. On reflection, I should have talked him back in and he might still be with us.

19th November 2020

The butcher in the supermarket seemed to be in a particularly cheerful mood today. Actually, it's time I stopped just calling him…' the butcher '. His name is Jacko…which I presume is an elongation of Jack, or perhaps a derivation of James.

Me : Morning, I'm looking for a nice shank of lamb.

Without warning, Jacko immediately burst into song. " Spring is in the air, every sight and every sound….spring is in the air, every…."

I was reluctant to point out that we were in the midst of winter. He then paused, trying to recall the second verse of the song which seemed to have deserted him. There followed a few seconds of awkward silence as his brain ticked over and his lips moved silently up and down in the hope that they might encourage the words to burst forth. But it was a forlorn hope.

Jacko : Any plans for today?

Me : No, nothing special…just taking it easy

Jacko : Take it..e…e…eeeeasy….

I recognised the first words of an old ' Eagles ' song but once again when it came to the second verse, Jacko's memory deserted him.

Jacko : Right, there we are, a lovely shank of lamb.

Jacko handed me the shank of lamb and then immediately adopted a posture, indicative of someone about to hold forth to an audience….eyes fixed straight ahead and both arms, with hands open palmed, half raised in the air. I thought initially that the first verse of another song was imminent. But I was wrong….it was poetry he had in mind.

"A shank of spring lamb

Only £14 per kilogram

A joy to behold

Of pleasures untold".

You seem in a particularly buoyant mood today, Jacko, I suggested to him.

Jacko : My wife cooked a vegan meal last night for both of us…

Me : And…?

Jacko : By God, it was bloody nice

Me : Good to hear…what was in it?

Jacko : Oh, God knows…damn nice though.

Me : You must ask her for the recipe. I'd like to give it a go myself sometime.

Jacko : Well, lets not get too carried away…I don't want to encourage her too much.

" Unexpected item in the bagging area! ".. " Unexpected item in the bagging area! "

Supermarket Manager : Excuse me, Sir, would you mind moving off the self scanning machine, please.

Me : Sorry, I just needed a bit of a sit down

23rd November 2020

I think I may have caught a bout of Covid 19. I have no energy, feel listless and tired all the time with sore joints and am blighted with a continuous gnawing pain in my stomach. Fortunately, I'm not suffering from shortness of breath and I don't seem to have any fever, not yet anyway. I suppose it could be the standard bout of flu, but if it is then it is the most severe bout of flu I have ever encountered. I receive a flu jab ever winter since I turned sixty over ten years ago and have never contracted the flu since, so it is more likely to be covid. I don't think I'll be posting anything in my diary for a few weeks anyway. Fortunately one of my sons lives nearby and is delivering food to me, although I have no great appetite for food apart from tinned fruit for some reason.

12th December 2020

I am at last feeling a bit better. I now know for sure it must have been a dose of covid because I have completely lost my sense of smell and my sense of taste is certainly nothing like it used to be. I'm told that they will both return in time, the time varying from person to person in length. I am nolonger sleeping for fourteen to fifteen hours at a time and mercifully the constant gnawing pain in my stomach has dissipated.

Here's to the future!

15th December 2020

I just HAD to buy this bunch of flowers today.

If you look closely enough at the photograph overleaf, you just might be able to see a feint image of my face in them.

Some people can see it, some can't!

23rd December 2020

It's Wednesday today and the time is 1.55pm. Maureen told me the last time we talked that she usually cleans her windows at 2 O'clock on Wednesdays. Firstly, three weeks have passed since that conversation and because of contracting the Covid virus I wasn't really in the mood for talking to anyone, let alone cleaning my windows. She was probably only joking anyway. But that still hasn't stopped me from pacing about my sitting room waiting for 2 O'clock to arrive so I can take my bucket of water and cleaning utensils to the window. This is ridiculous. I'm standing like a nervous child beside the window but out of sight. It's now 1.59pm. I must look casual when I go to the window and open it in preparation for cleaning.

"Don't look across at her window expectantly....if she's there, wait a couple of minutes before acknowledging her as if you've just noticed her....okay here we go!"

I'm now opening my window and studying it far too intensely for signs of dirt. I'm not looking outwards across the street, but a surreptitious side glance tells me that Maureen isn't at her window. I start to clean my window but I'm not even sure that it needs to be cleaned. It's now 2.10 pm and my window is gleaming like it has never done before. Still no sign of Maureen.

Maybe she's looking out at me from the interior of her room and laughing because she must know that I'm stalling at the window and that there is nothing more I can do to make my window more presentable.

"Wait a minute, there's movement just inside her window...it's opening!"

Maureen : Oh, hello there

Me: Hi, how's it going?

Maureen : All good, thanks....haven't seen you for a while.

Me : No, I had a dose of Covid for a few weeks.

Maureen : Oh, poor you....and there was I thinking you'd been standing me up.

The lockdown rules have been relaxed a bit for the Christmas period. Maureen and I chatted a bit more to the point that she invited me over to have a Christmas drink in her garden. It turned out that we are both very fond of red wine and had managed to get through a couple of bottles before the time reached 4pm.

Maureen : Oh shit, I've just remembered I don't have anything in for dinner....better get down to the supermarket
before I'm too drunk to walk.

Me : I'll get you down, I need some things myself.

We were both a bit tipsy by the time we arrived at the
supermarket, Maureen in particular I have to say. Perhaps
the fact that we were both wearing masks and therefore
continued to breathe in some alcoholic fumes when we
exhaled probably contributed to our state of inebriation.I
discovered that Christine is a bit of a raver after she's
downed a number of glasses of red wine. Christmas songs
were being played in a loop in the supermarket and as
we entered " Rockin' around the Christmas tree " was re-
verberating around the building. Christine got somewhat
carried away in the moment, enticing me to rock around
the Christmas tree with her, which had been positioned at
the side of the entrance to the supermarket. At one point
she spun around with too much verve, losing her balance,
and one of her arms became entangled with the Christmas
lights adorning the tree. Her momentum carried her away
from rather than toward the tree, which twirled and swiv-

elled before it came crashing to the floor in a crescendo of pine, Christmas lights and baubles. Miraculously, the Fairy at the top of the tree wasn't to be budged from its perch. I suspect that Maureen and I may have to find a new supermarket to shop in from now on.

When I arrived home later, the lyrics to "Rockin' around the Christmas tree." were still ringing in my head. Then a thought struck me...if musicians can write Christmas songs, why can't comedians create Christmas jokes? An hour or so later, the following joke came into my head....inspired by the famous 'Christmas song' by Wizard.

"Oh, I wish it could be Christmas everyday, which would mean there would have been 365 Jesus's and and it would place the Virgin Mary's chastity under much closer scrutiny. "

I doubt very much if my joke will upstage songs like "Fairytale of New York" but I'm going to post it up on my You Yube channel anyway. Who knows that in years to come, when the World has been plunged into some dystopian darkness and the population is ruled by an autocratic Council of ten members known as, "The Sanctus" who have banned all forms of music, that then my joke will be relayed into everyone's homes by The Sanctus every Christmas and played constantly over the intercom in supermarkets for the five weeks leading up to Christmas.

31st December 2020

Last night on the sauce before quitting for the New Year!

3rd January 2021

It is a new year, whatever that really means? Well, I suppose this is the first time in a long time since the birth of the aforementioned, Jesus, that it really is a New Year. A new year which has started in lockdown.

I went for a walk with Maureen along the Kelvin river in Glasgow yesterday afternoon. We seem to hit it off very well with each other and she has invited me to dinner at her flat at the weekend. I was telling her about my lockdown diary and she expressed an interest in reading it. Obviously I don't want to show her the entry when I was fretting about going to the window to reconvene our acquaintance, so I will leave that bit out when I send her a copy.

5th January 2021

If a fashion of 'mantlepiece posing' wearing Chelsea boots ever becomes a trend, I'm sure to make a fortune.

6th January 2020

There was quite a large crowd of people gathered outside the supermarket today when I arrived. There were all there cheering on the busker, whose name is Billy, by the way. It seems that his fame has spread far and wide.

When he'd finished playing the chords of Strawberry Fields on his guitar, intermingling the lyrics of Strawberry Fields with those of Penny Lane as he went, a huge roar of applause went up from the appreciative crowd, many of whom placed money in his hats...he now had two hats placed in front of him instead of one, obviously anticipating correctly that one would no longer suffice to hold all the booty that was coming his way.

Good luck to him!

7th January 2021

I was sucked into a ridiculous, heated argument with a neighbour today about when to take Christmas decorations down. He insisted on asking why I was taking them down and also how I'd managed to gain entry to his flat while he was out walking.

9th January 2021

I hope that I am not the only one that's remembered it's....'
NATIONAL BRING A JOCKEY TO WORK DAY.' today

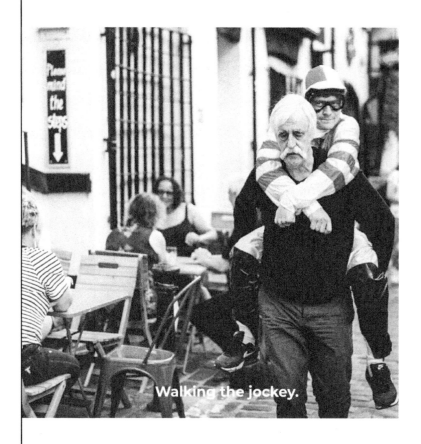

Walking the jockey.

11th January 2021

I got sucked into watching a documentary about ghosts on television last night which left us to decide for ourselves whether or not we believed in their existance. There were so called ' experts ' commenting on the matter , although none of them divulged the path they followed to arrive at a state of expertise on the subject of our disembodied friends. There were also interviews with people who considered themselves victims of evil spirited ghosts, which seemed unfair as the the ghosts had no right of reply.

I personally don't believe in the existance of ghostly creatures or spirits. However, should I ever be proved wrong, I can't deny that ghosts have an uncanny eye for the property market. You only ever hear of ghosts haunting the East or West wing of some large, country mansion in it's own grounds...I have yet to hear a commentary from the resident of a one bedroomed, damp ridden flat on the fourteenth floor of a Council scheme about ghostly visitations.

14th January 2021

Tonight is the night of my dinner date with Maureen. I am incredibly nervous on two counts. Firstly, I have not been on a date for a long time and am worried that I will be out of practice, not that I was ever a particularly smooth practitioner of social interaction. It has become clear over the past few weeks that Maureen and I hit it off with each other, but this is the first time we're going on an actual date...or is it even a date? Maybe I'm just assuming it is but from her point of view she is simply inviting a neighbour to dinner whose company she happens to enjoy.

Secondly, I emailed her an attachment of the first 50 pages of my book/diary two days ago. She hasn't responded by email to give me her take on it. Perhaps she hasn't read it yet...or perhaps she has and didn't take to it at all or is she waiting to tell me tonight that she loves it! I think I need to stop fretting and just take the night as it comes.

Right, here goes. I ring the doorbell of her flat, announce myself and she presses the buzzer to allow me entry into the building. She is waiting at the door to her flat as I arrive up the stairs.

Maureen : Fucks' sake, you're a minute early...I was just about to drain the carrots.

I immediately felt the tension lift from my shoulders as she sat me down and plonked a large glass of red wine on the table in front of me. We chatted easily about this and that for a while but as each minute passed I began to wonder more and more if she was going to mention my book. She left the room briefly to check on something in the kitchen and returned to say that dinner would be ready very soon.

Maureen : Oh, I only had time to read the first 30 pages or so of your book...read it in bed last night...loved it, I think it's hilarious.

Me : Oh, that's... great, thanks.

I think she may have spotted the expression of relief on my face.

Maureen : Don't look so surprised....can't wait to read the rest of it.

Without going into details, the rest of the evening went brilliantly well.

24th January 2021

I can understand why some people think it's a bit strange that I keep two shop mannequins in my flat. They didn't arrive in the flat as part of a devised plan on my part. I acquired the first mannikin a few years ago when a friend of mine who'd owned a clothes shop had decided to sell up. I was helping him to clean out his shop one day and as I lifted up one of the mannikins, the thought struck me of how life-like it was and I couldn't bring myself to throw it into the skip. I came across the second one a couple of months later while visiting a local charity shop who were about to discard the mannikin because a piece of the polystyrene holding its head to its upper body had become warped. As a result, the mannequin's head was permanently tilted to one side, leaving it with the posture of someone who had never properly recovered from a particularly nasty accident. Since this particular mannikin was female and the original one which I'd acquired was male, I thought it would be a good idea to address the mannikin gender balance in my flat.

'Madeleine' has now joined 'Bob' in my hallway, each in separate corners, standing facing each other. I have dressed Madeleine in a fake fur coat, trailing to her ankles, and have also adorned her face with a pair of sunglasses. Bob is attired in a pair of workmens' overalls. They are an unlikely couple.

Checkout Assistant : Hi there.

Me : Hi.

Checkout Assistant : Doing some DIY today?

Me : DIY?...oh, the Polyfilla....no, no, it's for one of my mannikins. A piece of her neck is a bit squiffy and needs to be built up a bit.

Checkout Assistant : Oh, I see...so you own a clothes shop?

Me : No, I just have a couple of mannequins in my flat.

Checkout Assistant : In your flat?

Me : Yes....Bob and Madeleine.

Checkout Assistant : ......£19.24 when you're ready please

30th January 2021

I saw an item on the news today that scientists in NASA think they may have detected a planet in a different galaxy to ours which could provide conditions similar to Earth and so be able to nurture intelligent life. Naturally, it's speculative and will not be proven one way or another until many years to come as the planet is light years away in distance. I didn't catch how many light years away it is but let's just say it's a hell of a long way...I hope my terminology of distances in space travel is not too technical for you.

However, this information set my mind to thought. What if in 200/300 years time, NASA does create a spacecraft capable of travelling to this other galaxy and landing on the planet in question. Despite the increased level of technology, I imagine it would still take a considerable time to complete the journey..let us say, for example, it takes 5 years. After 5 years of a long and arduous journey for the astronauts, the spacecraft reaches and lands on the planet. However, imagine a scenario whereby after all that travelling, combined with enormous expectation, that they don't discover intelligent life on the planet at all. Instead they find themselves on a planet inhabited by feckin' eejits. People with heads far too big for the rest of their body to support ,playing football in a nearby field, using an over-grown turnip as a football and as the astronauts are climbing down the ladder from the spacecraft, there is already a guy standing at the bottom urinating, holding a rottweiler on a lead in one hand and a half eaten hamburger in the other one. The leading astronaut looks down on the scene before him and thinks…"Oh, for Christ's sake! 5 years of travelling to be met by this…we could have seen the same thing on a weekend in Scunthorpe"

8th February 2021

My relationship with Maureen is now in full flow. I was about to write that we are officially boyfriend and girl-friend, but since I am 71 years old and she is in her sixties, I suppose it's more applicable to call us man friend and woman friend. No!, that doesn't sound right either...any-way, you know what I mean.

Our degree of intimacy has reached the stage that when I met her in the street yesterday on my way to the dentists, I had occasion to give her my flat keys. As I say, I was on the way to the dentist's but she was on her way home. Just before we'd bumped into each other, I'd had a panicky thought that I'd left a ring on my cooker on, so I'd asked her if she wouldn't mind popping into my flat to check on it.

My visit to the dentists wasn't too stressful. It was really just a check up but he did insist on performing that clean-ing action on my teeth with that instrument that looks a bit like a fish hook and on occasion finds a nerve, causing you to shudder suddenly in the same way a fish does when it tries to pull away from the hook.

I happily made my way home, first calling in to Maureen's

to collect my keys back from her. I rang her bell a couple of times but there was no response. I then waited a few minutes in case she was in the bathroom or engaged in some other task, disabling her to answer the doorbell. But still no response to the doorbell after another five minutes. I was beginning to worry a little at this stage and decided to ring her phone. It rang three or four times and then was answered by this male voice which I didn't recognise.

Me : Hello...who's this?

Man : Oh hello, is that Michael?

My worst fears were beginning to come to the surface.

"Yes, it is." I replied nervously, is something wrong with...?

"It's okay, Maureen's okay....she just had a bit of a shock, that's all."

Me : Oh, what happened?

Man : Are you still at the dentist's?

Me : No, I'm just outside Maureens' flat...she has my keys.

Man : Hold on a sec, we're in your flat...I'll buzz you up.

I walked over to my building, still puzzled and concerned about what had happened to Maureen. I walked up the stairs and was met at the door by my neighbour, Andy, who lives in the flat across the landing from me.

There were two things I'd neglected to warn Maureen about. Firstly, the light in my hallway needed a new bulb. My hallway can be a little dark, even in the day time, unless there is light coming from the sitting room or my bedroom but the doors to each had been closed over. Secondly, and no doubt more importantly, I had never mentioned to Maureen about Bob and Madeleine, my two mannikins. I hadn't deliberately avoided telling her about them. I'd just never got round to it. It transpired that Maureen had entered my flat and seconds later had walked straight into Bob in the darkness, who had seemed to her, without close examination, to be a stranger lurking in the shadows of my hallway. She'd run out of the flat screaming, attracting the attention of the aforementioned Andy. When I entered my flat, Maureen was sitting on my sofa, cradling a glass of brandy in her hand. Actually, I'm not sure if cradling is the right word in the circumstances, as we associate the action of cradling with a gentle soothing motion. Her hand was still shaking wildly as she raised the glass of brandy to her lips. Naturally, I offered my profuse apologies to her and tried to console her as best I could.

I hope our relationship survives this setback.

12th February 2021

I've already warned my toaster 14 times that if it mutilates one more slice of bread and traps it inside...IT'S GETTING IT!

19th February 2021

At my age you would think I should be more mature in the matters of romance. I opened my sitting room window today to air the room but as I did I noticed and heard Maureen engaged in some playful badinage from her sitting room window with Andy, my neighbour and her rescuer from a week or so before. They were both in the act of cleaning their windows as Maureen laughed heartily at some quip that Andy had just made. She must have seen me opening my window but she still didn't divert her eyes from Andy as her ripples of laughter floated in teasing waves across the street.

Why is she cleaning her windows today....it's not Wednesday today, it's Sunday, and it's not even near 2 0' clock. Has she been two-timing me all along and flirting with Andy every Sunday at this time from their sitting room windows. And was that why he was so quick to rescue her from her ordeal with Bob, my mannikin? Perhaps she's concluded that someone who entertains not just one but two mannikins in their flat, is not someone she would like to pursue a friendship with, let alone a relationship. Furthermore, she still hasn't responded to my text which I sent to her last night.

I realise that I am acting in a pathetic manner but despite that, the matter continues to niggle me. I've decided to call over to her later in the day and talk the issue over with her.

25th February 2021

I'd just left my flat to go to the supermarket and was opening the door to the street when I was greeted by Maureen who was just about to ring my doorbell.

Maureen : Oh, Hi, I was just about to..

Me : Hi, how are things?

Maureen : Fine, except I dropped my phone in the street on Saturday and it's completely banjaxed.

Me : That explains it…I sent you a text a couple of days ago but…

Maureen : Yeah, sorry, been meaning to call over but needed to visit my Aunt who is a bit ill…she's okay now but I didn't want to leave her alone.

Me : Good, glad to hear she's okay.

Maureen : Thanks….so, how are your mannikins, hope they've got over my screaming fit.

Her jokey remark about the mannikins cleared the air thankfully and she's coming over for dinner tomorrow. I made my way to the supermarket with a bit of a spring in my step.

Me : I'm in the mood for one of your fillet steaks.

Butcher: Oh, celebrating something?

Me : Well..not quite celebrating as such.

Butcher : I'm certainly not in a mood to celebrate.

Me : Oh, why's that?

Butcher : Got a call from the wife just before I was finishing up work yesterday…tells me to come along after work to meet her at this vegan cafe she'd found.

Me : And was it good?

Butcher : It might have been if I'd got the chance to eat in it.

Me : What do you mean…what happened?

Butcher : Well, I rushed out of work because a couple of customers had come in at the last minute and I was running a bit late…God Almighty, what a hullabaloo…in the rush I'd forgotten to take off my soiled butchers' apron…

Me : Oh dear..

Butcher: Owner of the vegan cafe shouted at me to get out immediately and one woman at a table was actually screaming.

Me : That sounds bad...what did your wife do?

Butcher : I hadn't sat down at the table yet so she just ignored me...looked down at her food as if I didn't exist... bloody awful it was......anyway, enjoy your fillet!

So, that's a year in lockdown with no real sign of it lifting.

Would I have met Maureen if it hadn't been for lockdown?...who knows!

I probably wouldn't have come up with the idea for my photographs because lockdown afforded me the opportunity and time to experiment a bit more with my comedy output and also to bring some stories to light.

Would I have found myself sitting in Jacko the butchers' house as I was yesterday evening with Maureen enjoying a vegan meal with Jacko and his wife?...probably not!

Finally in summing up, I can confirm that all the kidnapped jockeys are now back safe in Jockey Town and that the culprits have been arrested on charges of jockey trafficking and kidnapping.

Printed in Great Britain
by Amazon